P9-ELU-349

# THE NIGHT BEFORE CHRISTMAS

# THE NIGHT BEFORE
# CHRISTMAS

## TOLD IN SIGNED ENGLISH

An adaptation of the original poem "A Visit from St. Nicholas" by Clement C. Moore

Harry Bornstein
Karen Luczak Saulnier

Illustrated by Steve Marchesi

Sign Drawings by Jan Skrobisz

FOREST HOUSE ™
School & Library Edition

**Kendall Green Publications**
Gallaudet University Press
Washington, D.C.

Kendall Green Publications
An imprint of Gallaudet University Press, Washington, DC 20002
©1994 by Gallaudet University. All rights reserved

Printed in Singapore

Book design by Sharon Davis Thorpe, Panache Designs

*Library of Congress Cataloging-in-Publication Data*

Moore, Clement Clarke, 1779-1863.
    The night before Christmas : an adaptation of the original poem "A visit from St. Nicholas"
    by Clement C. Moore / Harry Bornstein, Karen Luczak Saulnier; illustrated by Steve Marchesi;
    sign drawings by Jan Skrobicz.
        p.      cm.
    ISBN I-56368-020-3
    1. Santa Claus-Juvenile poetry. 2. American Sign Language-Juvenile literature. 3. Children's
    poetry, American. 4. Christmas-Juvenile poetry. (1. Santa Claus-Poetry. 2. Christmas-Poetry.
    3. American poetry. 4. Narrative poetry. 5. Sign language.) I. Bornstein, Harry. II. Saulnier,
    Karen Luczak. III. Marchesi, Steve, ill. IV. Skrobisz, Jan, ill. V.Title.
    PS2429.M5N5   1994d
    811'.2-dc20                                   94-11477
                                                       CIP
                                                       AC

# To Parents and Teachers

The first printing of *The Night Before Christmas Told in Signed English* appeared in 1973. Parents and teachers, delighted to have a special version of this famous poem to share with deaf, hard-of-hearing, and language-delayed children, greeted it with a great deal of enthusiasm. Since the book was designed for very young children, we chose a simplified rendition of the poem for our text. However, in this 1994 edition, we present a more traditional wording of the poem almost exactly faithful to that written by Clement C. Moore in 1822.

Using the original text meant dealing with some obscure and infrequently encountered words, such as *coursers* and *droll*. No specific Signed English signs exist for these words due to their rarity of use. We have represented them in this book by Signed English signs with which they are conceptually compatible. For example, we've used the Signed English sign for *reindeer* to represent the word *coursers* and a variation of the Signed English sign for *funny* to stand for the word *droll*. One also can fingerspell these unusual words but doing so may interfere with the poem's cadence.

We encourage parents and teachers to recite and sign the poem just as it was written to allow children to experience the full wonder and magic of Dr. Moore's masterpiece. Children of all ages who are interested in sign for whatever reason can enjoy this unique interpretation of an important and delightful piece of American literature.

# American Manual Alphabet

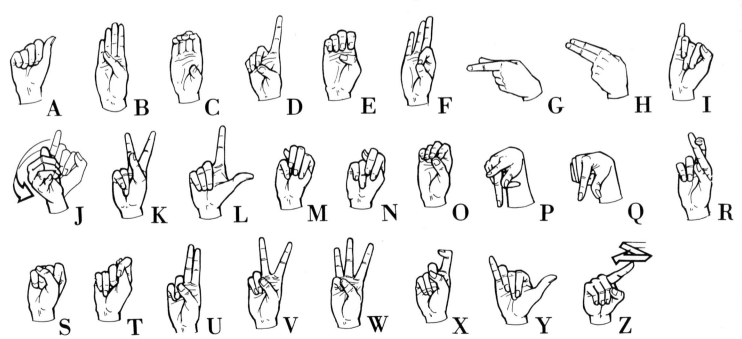

'Twas the night before Christmas, when all through the house Not a creature was stirring, not even a mouse;

[It]    was    the    night    before    Christmas,

when    all    through    the    house

Not a creature was stirring,

not even a mouse;

The stockings were hung
by the chimney with care,
In hopes that Saint Nicholas
soon would be there.

The          stockings          were          hung

by          the          chimney          with          care,

In          hopes          that          Saint          Nicholas

soon          would          be          there.

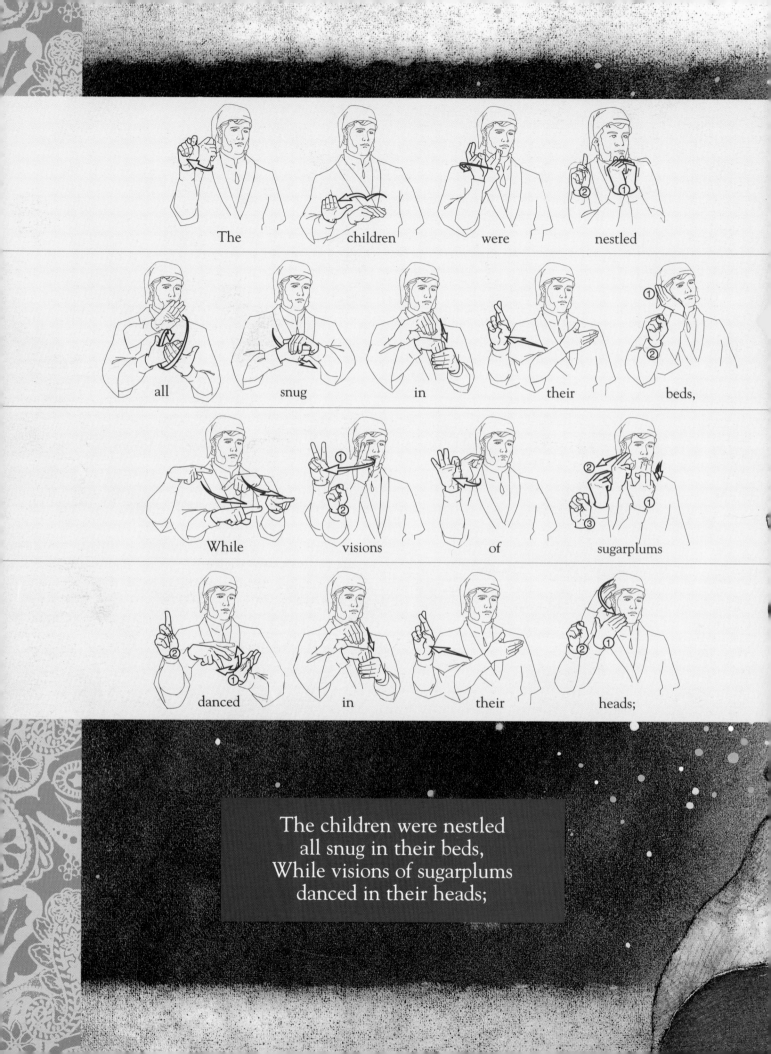

The children were nestled
all snug in their beds,
While visions of sugarplums
danced in their heads;

And Mama in her kerchief,
and I in my cap,
Had just settled down
for a long winter's nap,

And      Mama      in      her      kerchief,

and      I      in      my      cap,

Had      just      settled      down

for      a      long      winter's      nap,

When out on the lawn

there arose such a clatter

When out on the lawn
there arose such a clatter,
I sprang from my bed
to see what was the matter.

I sprang from my bed to

see what was the matter

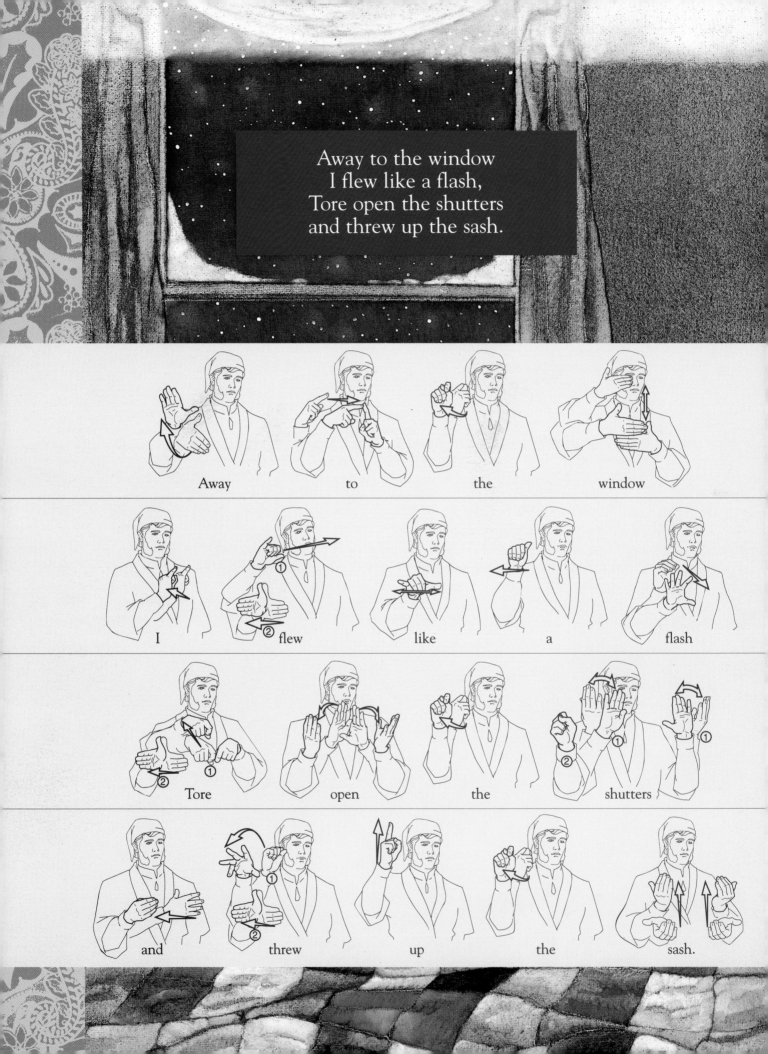

Away to the window
I flew like a flash,
Tore open the shutters
and threw up the sash.

Away　　to　　the　　window

I　　flew　　like　　a　　flash

Tore　　open　　the　　shutters

and　　threw　　up　　the　　sash.

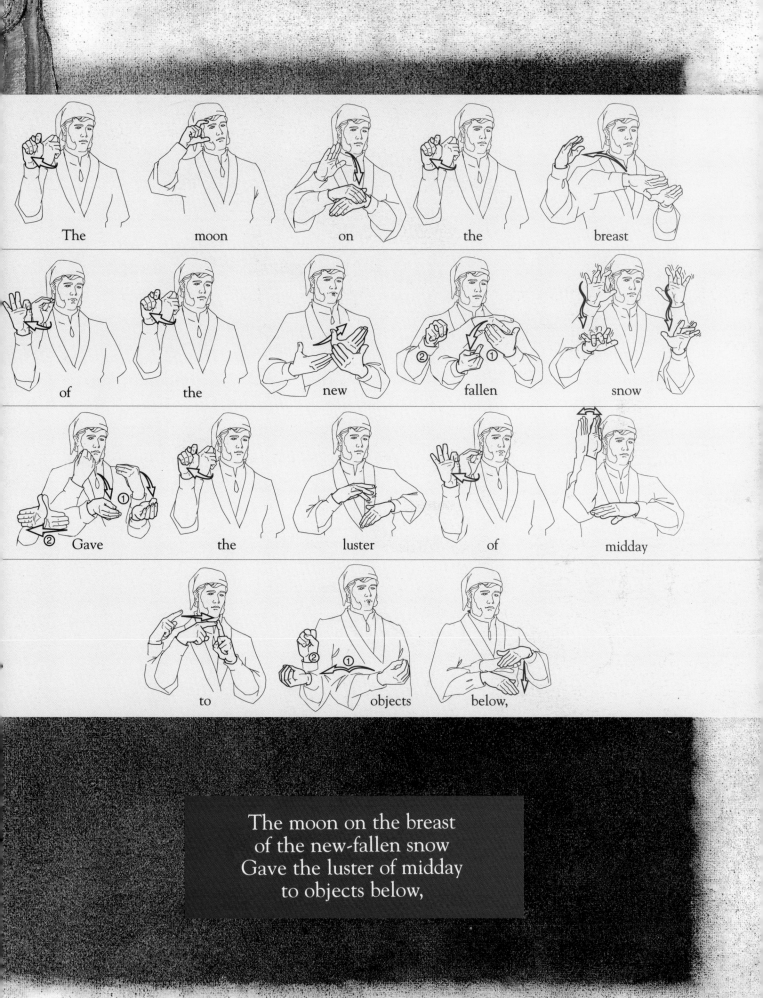

The moon on the breast
of the new-fallen snow
Gave the luster of midday
to objects below,

When what to my wondering
eyes should appear,
But a miniature sleigh
and eight tiny reindeer,

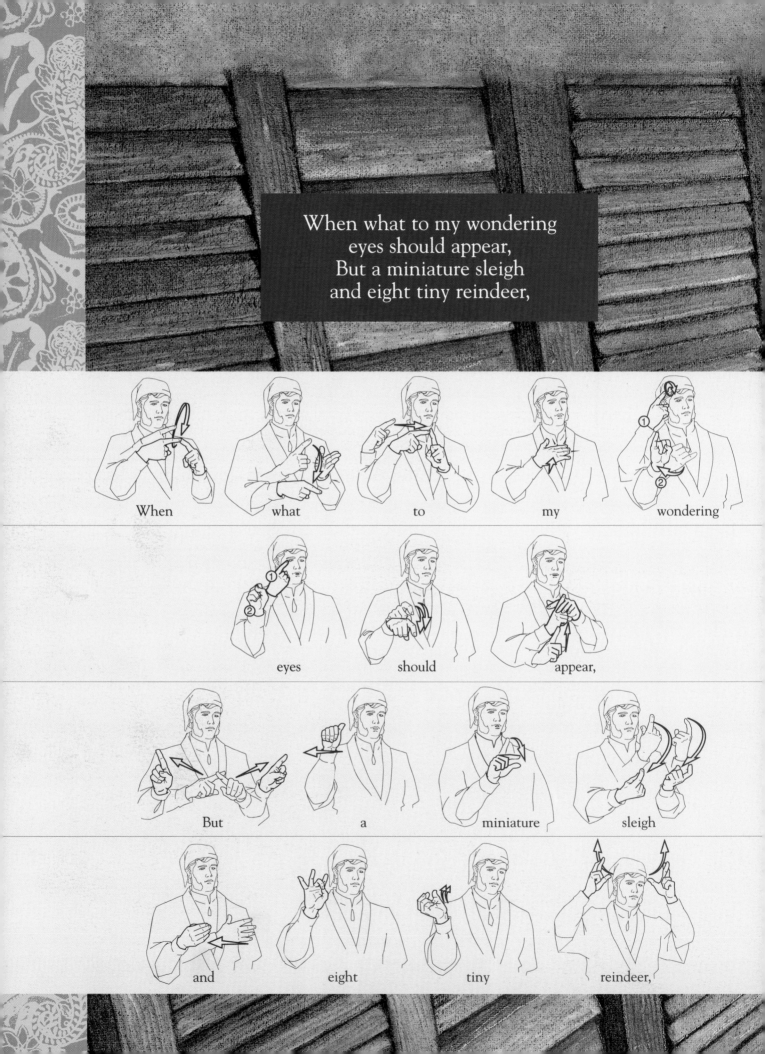

When    what    to    my    wondering

eyes    should    appear,

But    a    miniature    sleigh

and    eight    tiny    reindeer,

With a little old driver

so lively and quick,

With a little old driver,
so lively and quick,
I knew in a moment
It must be Saint Nick.

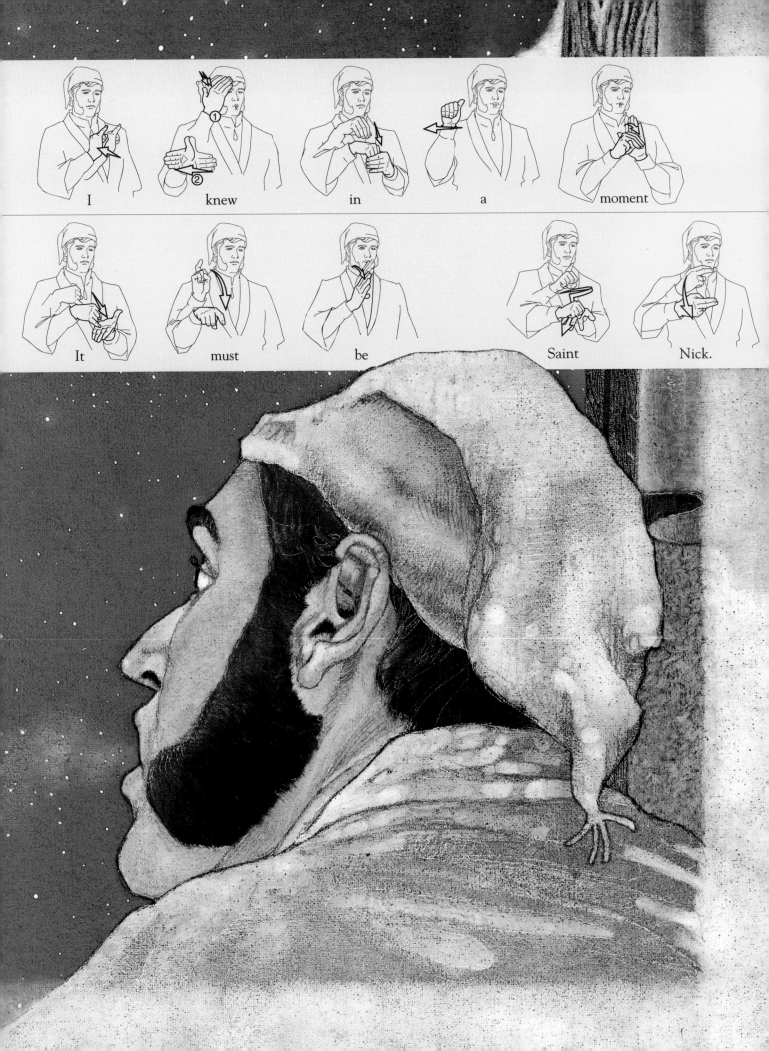

I knew in a moment

It must be Saint Nick.

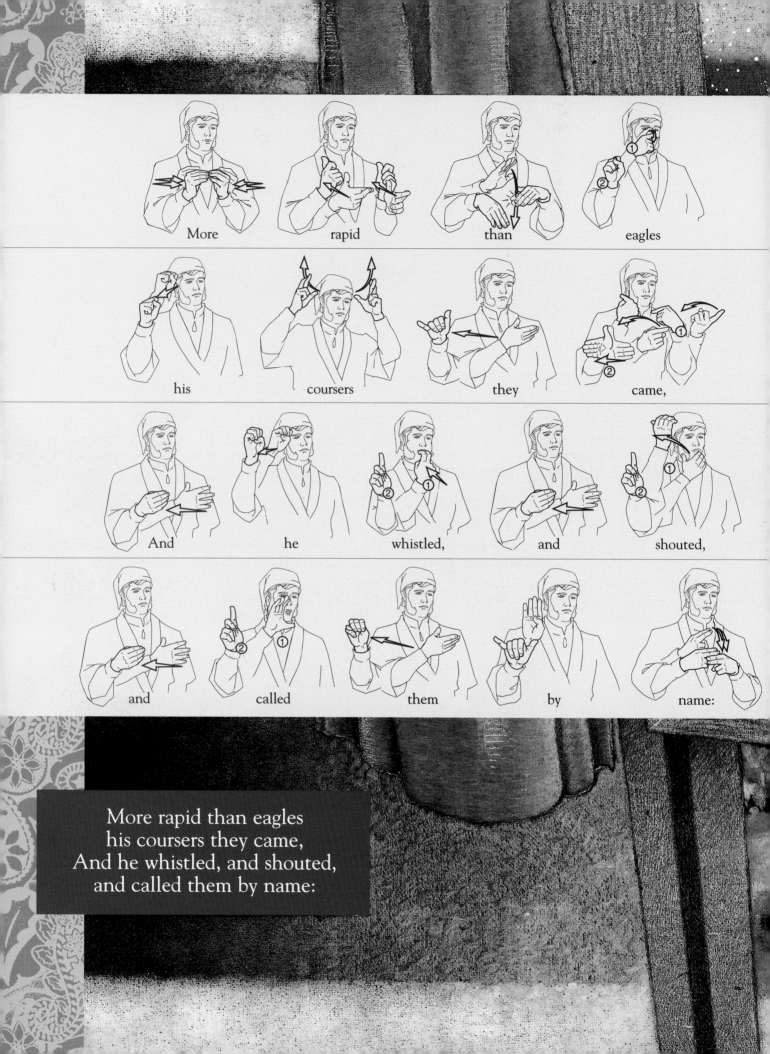

More rapid than eagles
his coursers they came,
And he whistled, and shouted,
and called them by name:

"Now, Dasher! now Dancer!
Now, Prancer and Vixen!
On, Comet! on, Cupid!
On, Donner and Blitzen!

"Now,     Dasher!     now     Dancer!

Now,     Prancer     and     Vixen!

On,     Comet!     on,     Cupid!

On,     Donner     and     Blitzen!

To the top of the porch!
to the top of the wall!
Now, dash away! dash away!
dash away, all!"

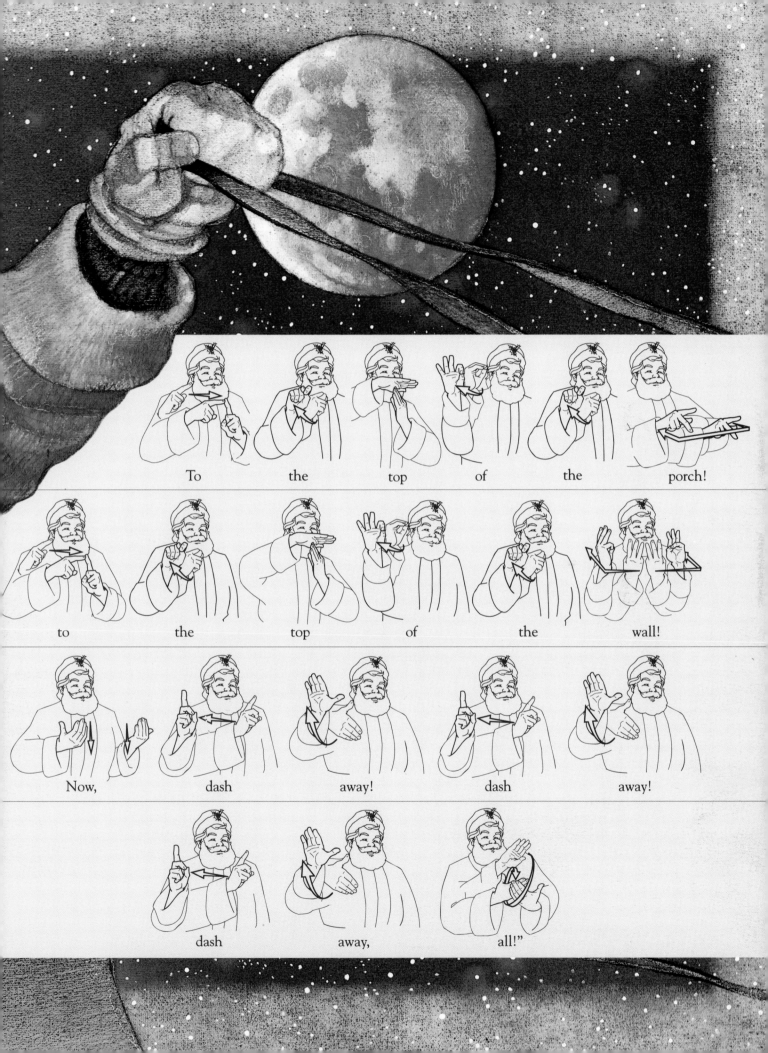

To the top of the porch!

to the top of the wall!

Now, dash away! dash away!

dash away, all!"

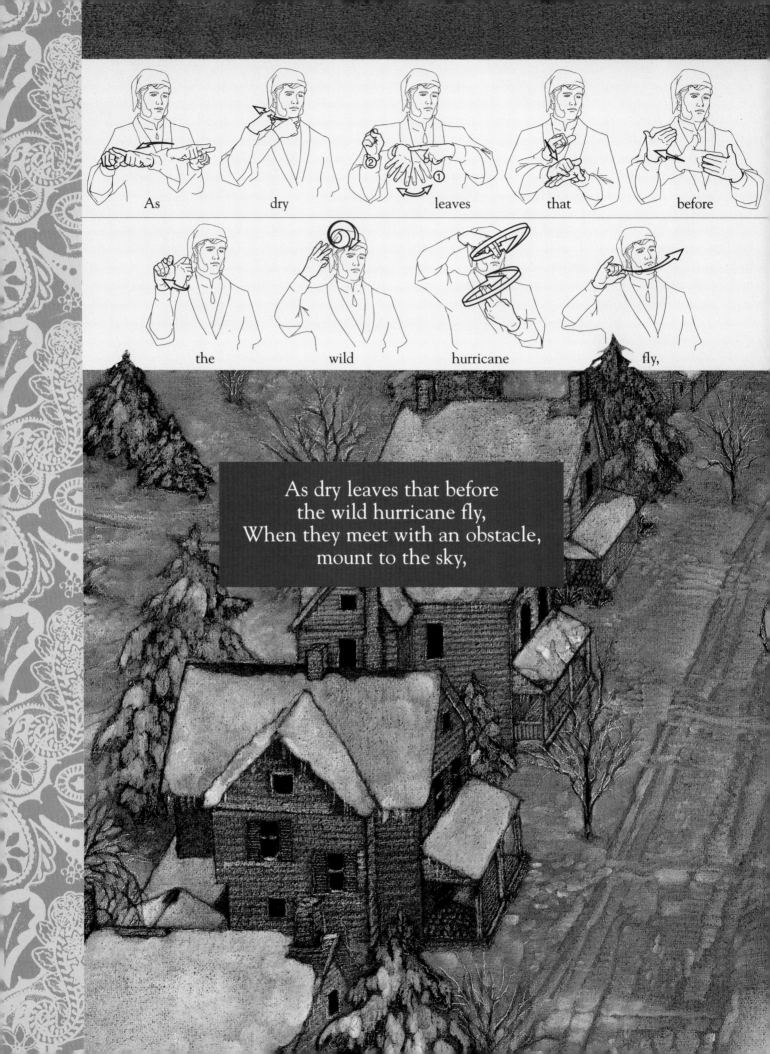

As dry leaves that before
the wild hurricane fly,
When they meet with an obstacle,
mount to the sky,

When they meet with an obstacle,

mount to the sky,

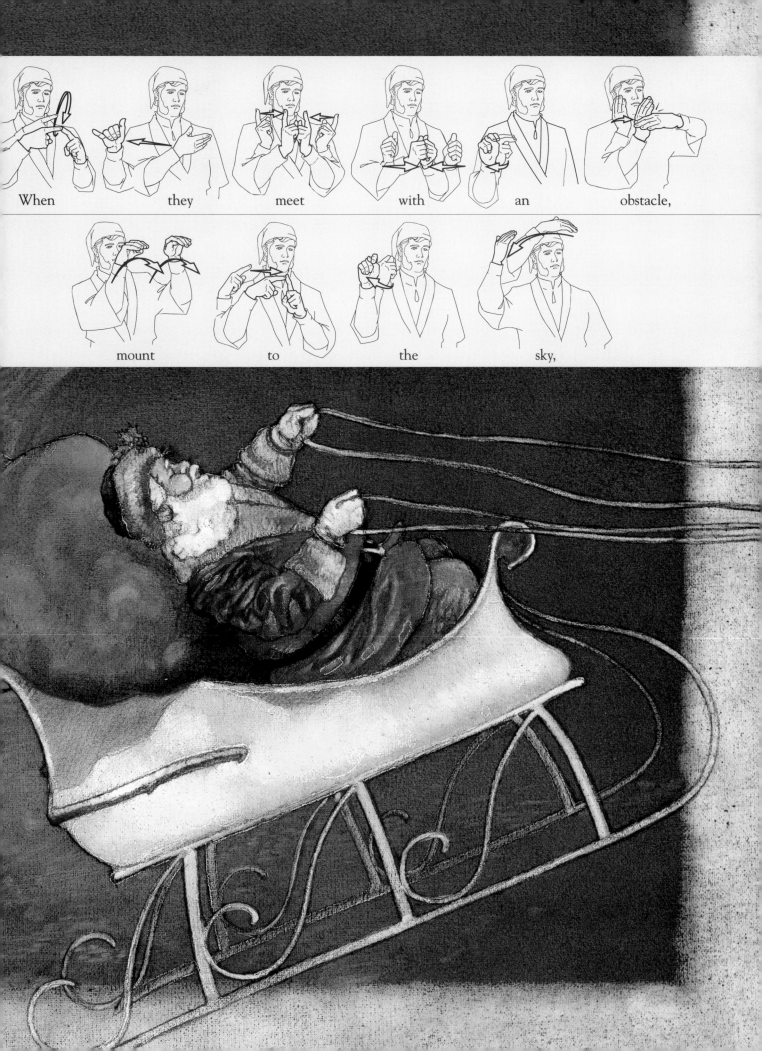

So up to the housetop
the coursers they flew,
With a sleigh full of toys,
and Saint Nicholas, too.

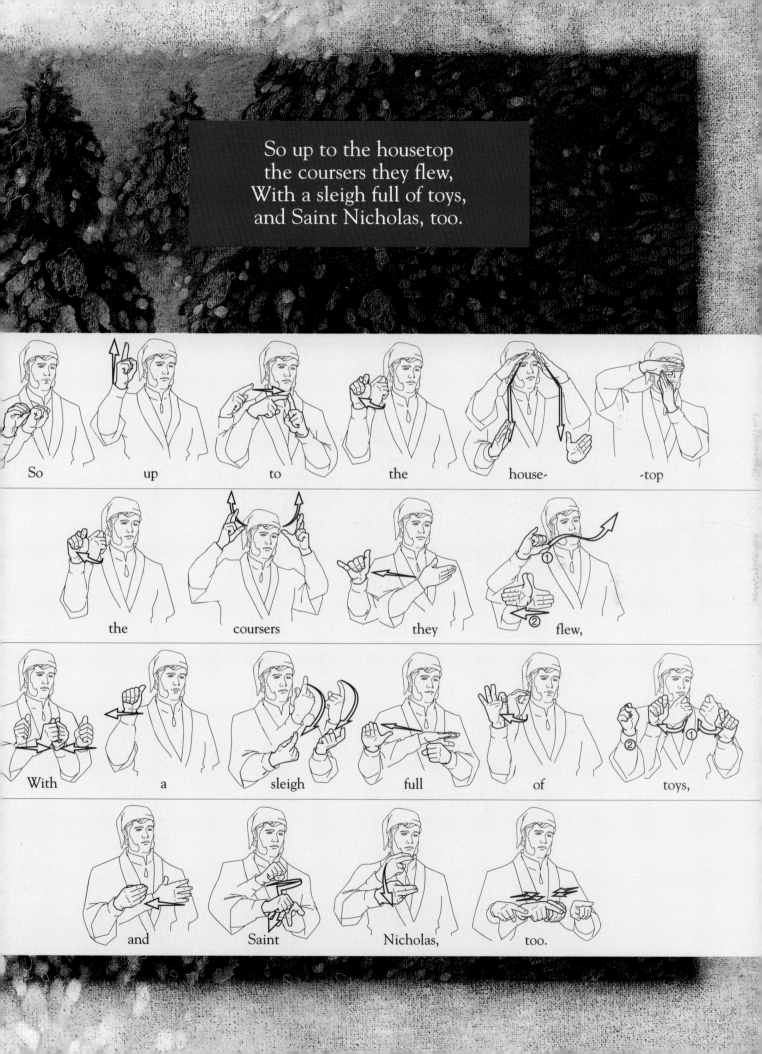

So     up     to     the     house-     -top

the     coursers     they     flew,

With     a     sleigh     full     of     toys,

and     Saint     Nicholas,     too.

And then, in a twinkling,
I heard on the roof
The prancing and pawing
of each little hoof.

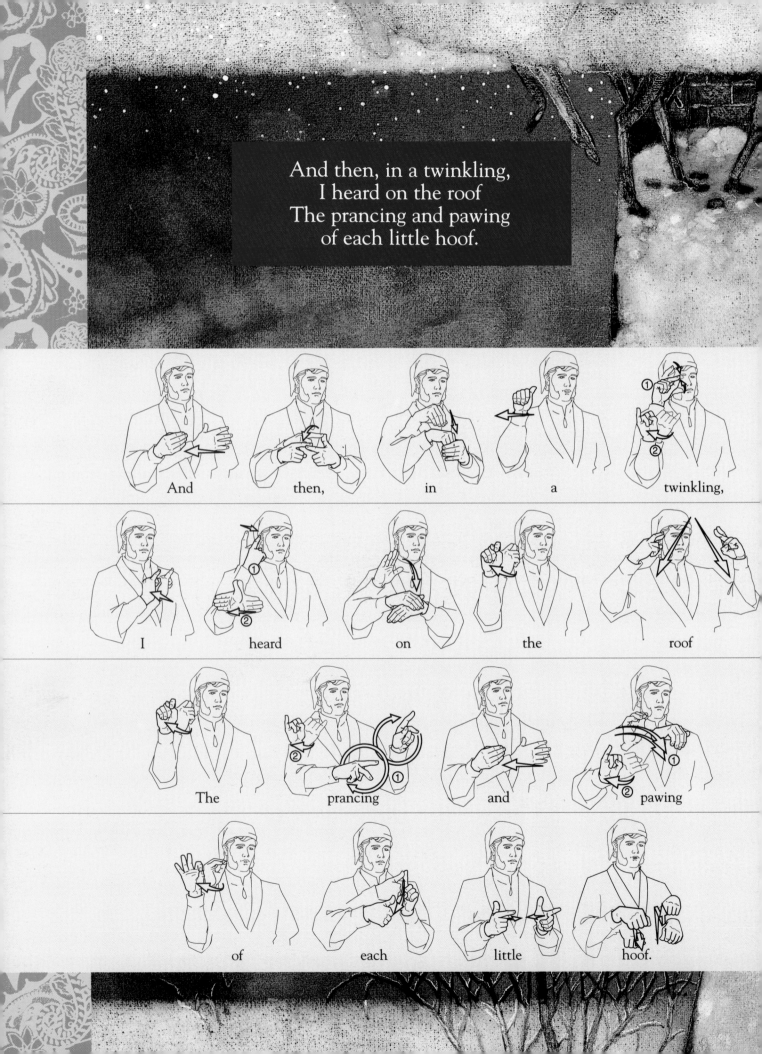

And        then,        in        a        twinkling,

I        heard        on        the        roof

The        prancing        and        pawing

of        each        little        hoof.

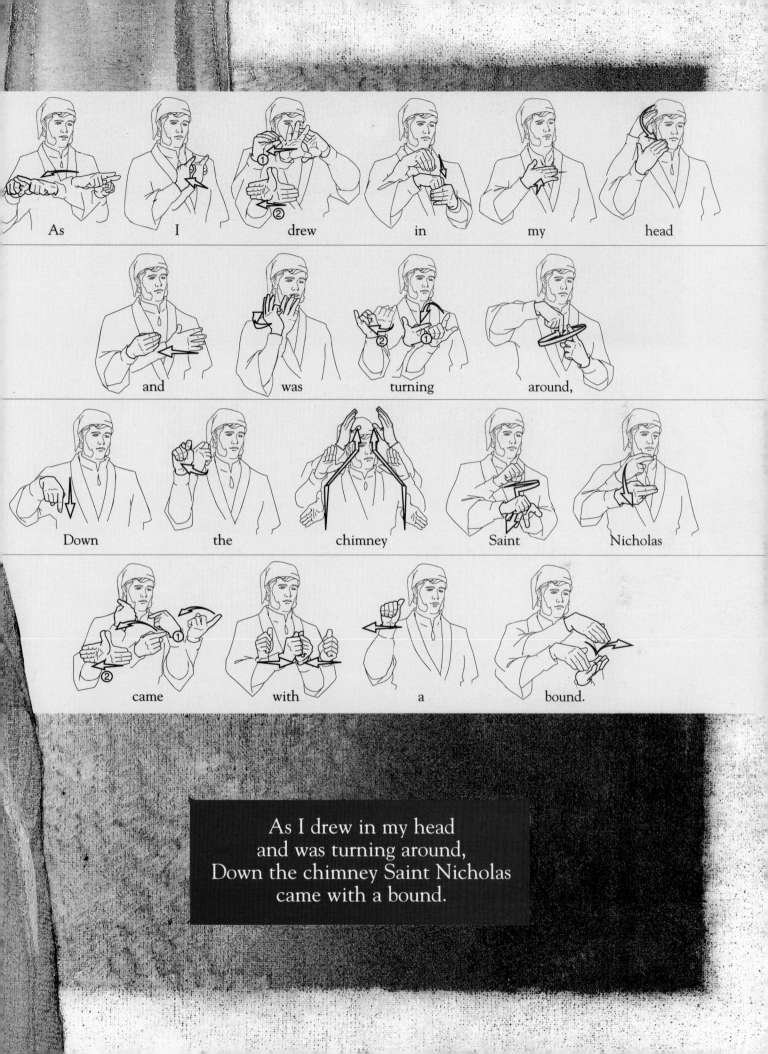

As I drew in my head
and was turning around,
Down the chimney Saint Nicholas
came with a bound.

He was dressed all in fur,
from his head to his foot,
And his clothes were all tarnished
with ashes and soot;

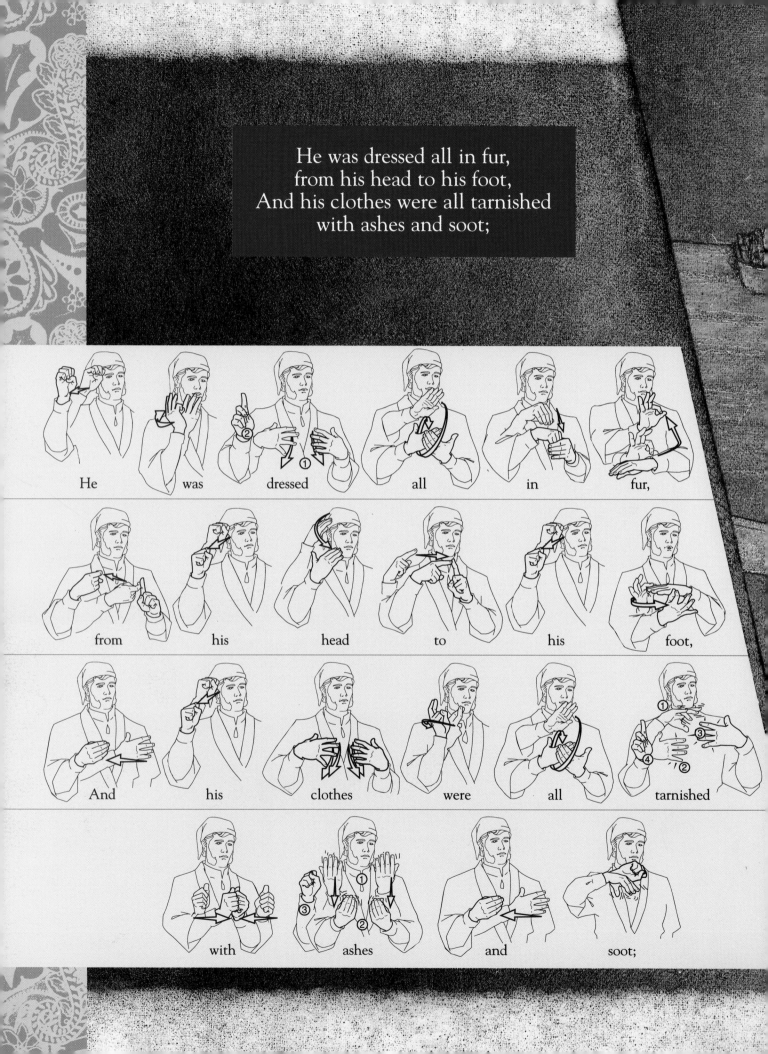

He    was    dressed    all    in    fur,

from    his    head    to    his    foot,

And    his    clothes    were    all    tarnished

with    ashes    and    soot;

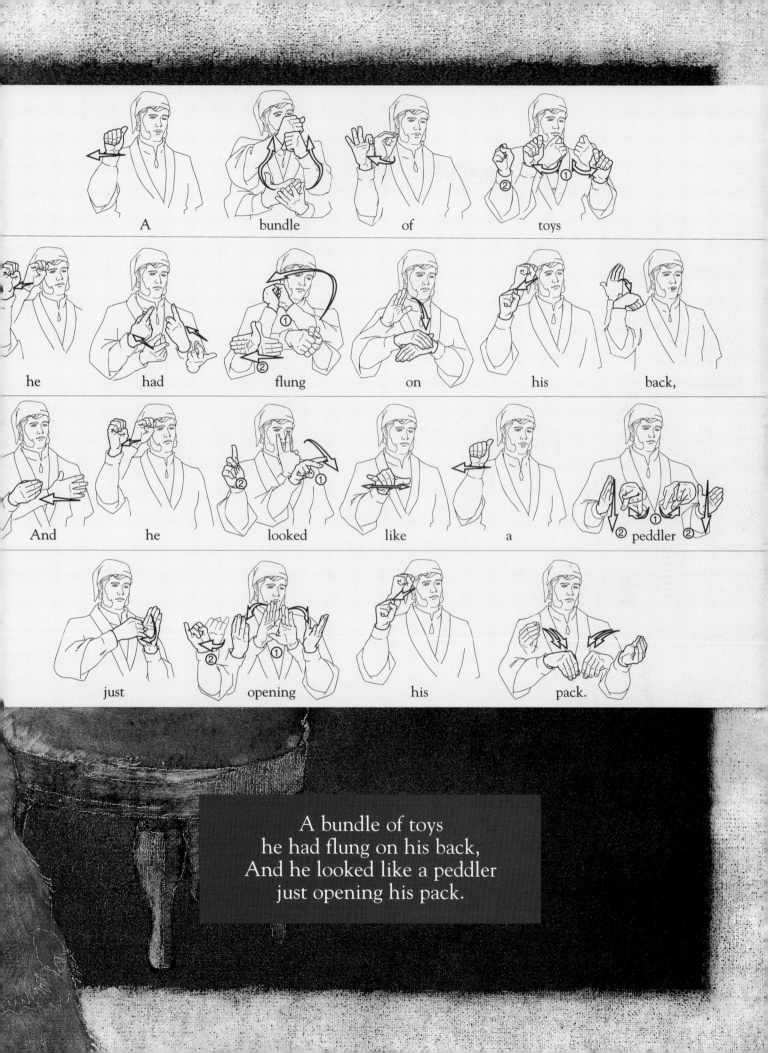

A bundle of toys
he had flung on his back,
And he looked like a peddler
just opening his pack.

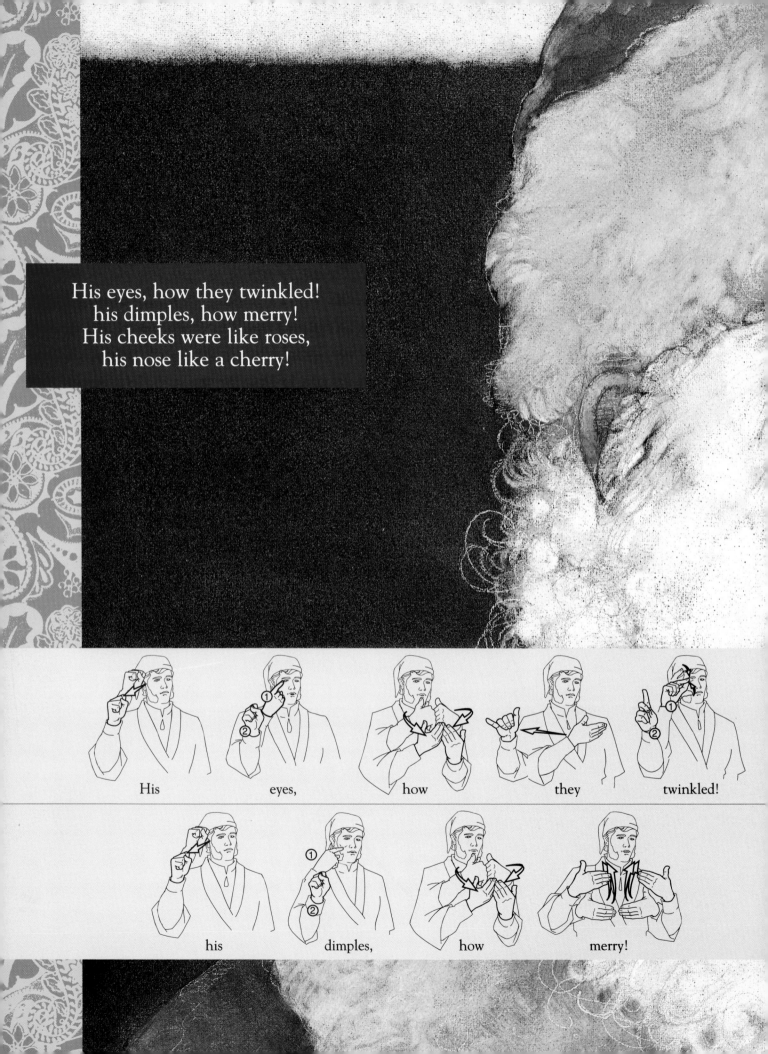

His eyes, how they twinkled!
his dimples, how merry!
His cheeks were like roses,
his nose like a cherry!

His eyes, how they twinkled!

his dimples, how merry!

His       cheeks       were       like       roses,

his       nose       like       a       cherry!

His droll little mouth
was drawn up like a bow,
And the beard on his chin
was as white as the snow.

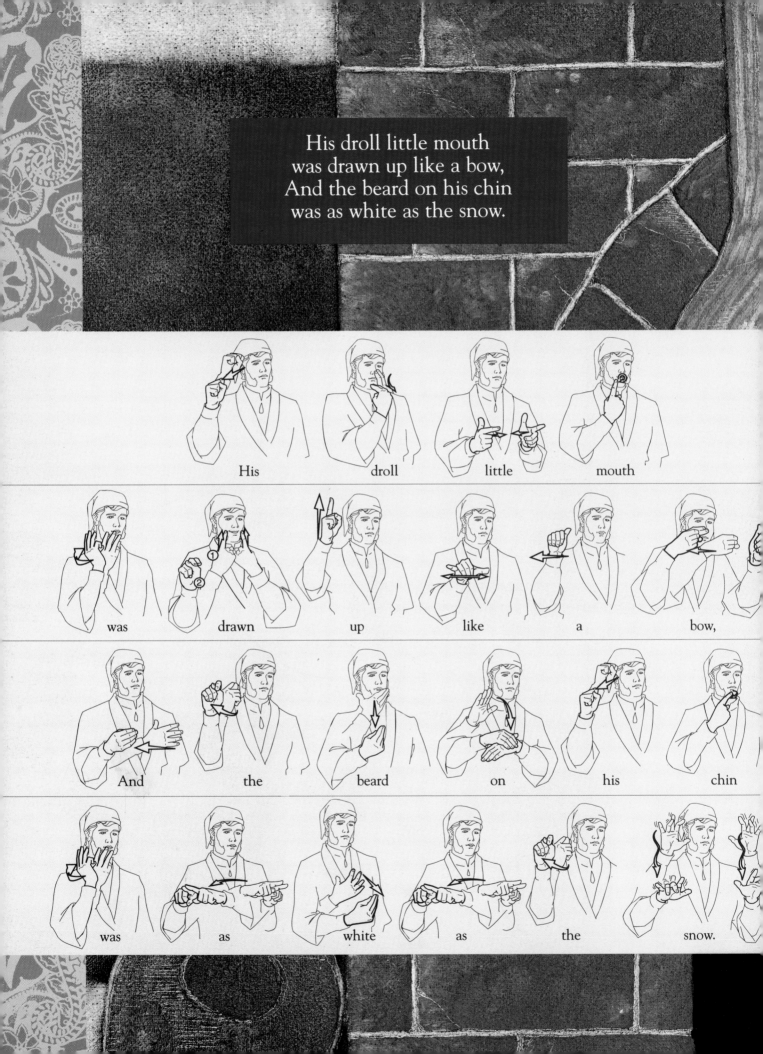

His     droll     little     mouth

was     drawn     up     like     a     bow,

And     the     beard     on     his     chin

was     as     white     as     the     snow.

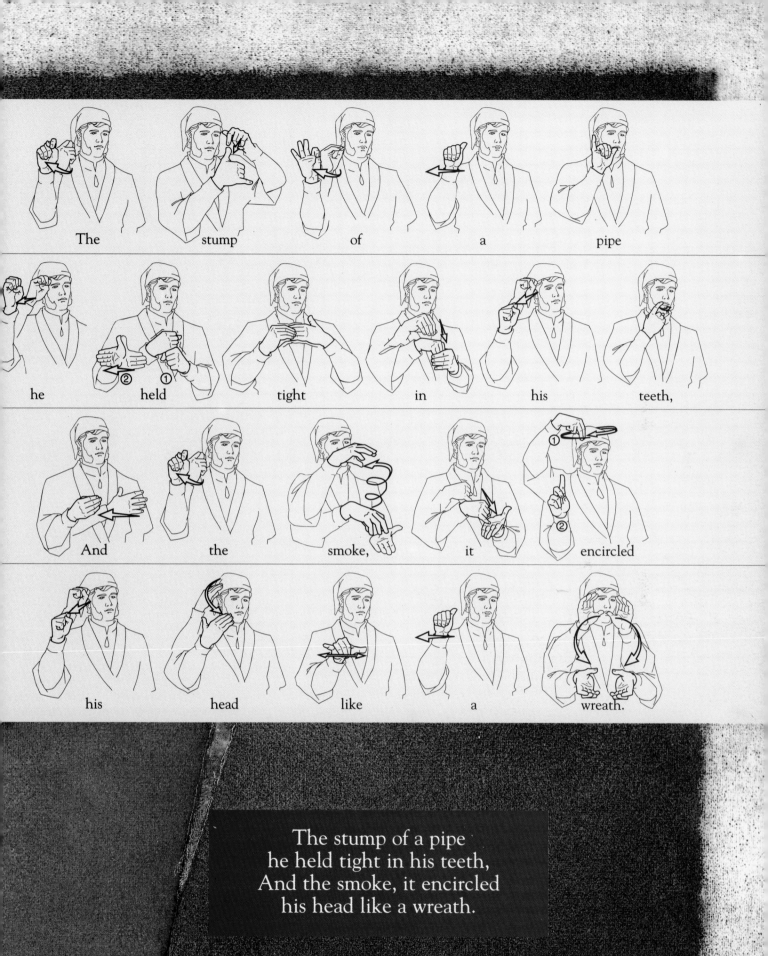

The stump of a pipe
he held tight in his teeth,
And the smoke, it encircled
his head like a wreath.

He had a broad face
and a little round belly
That shook when he laughed,
like a bowl full of jelly.

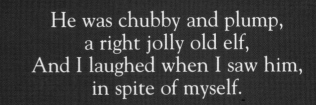

He was chubby and plump,
a right jolly old elf,
And I laughed when I saw him,
in spite of myself.

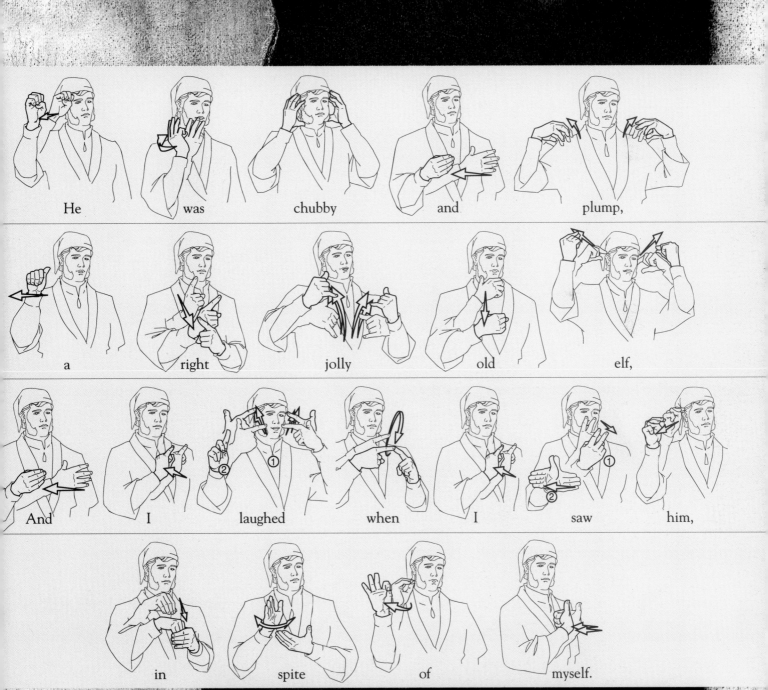

He    was    chubby    and    plump,

a    right    jolly    old    elf,

And    I    laughed    when    I    saw    him,

in    spite    of    myself.

A wink of his eye
and a twist of his head
Soon gave me to know
I had nothing to dread.

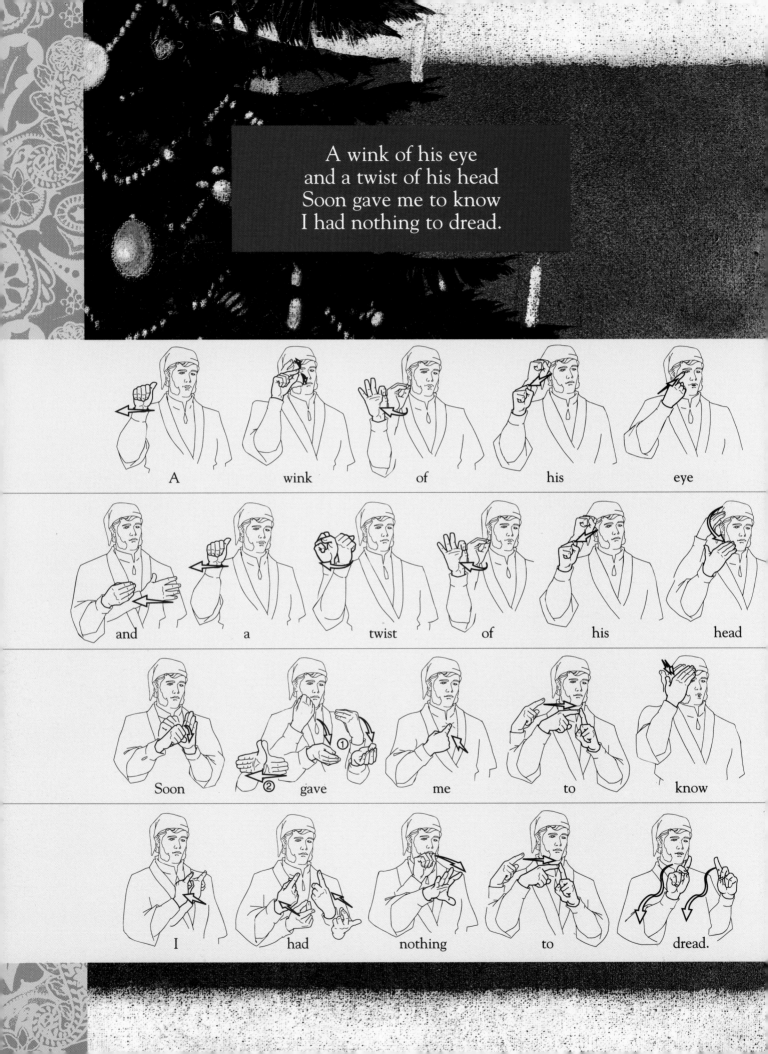

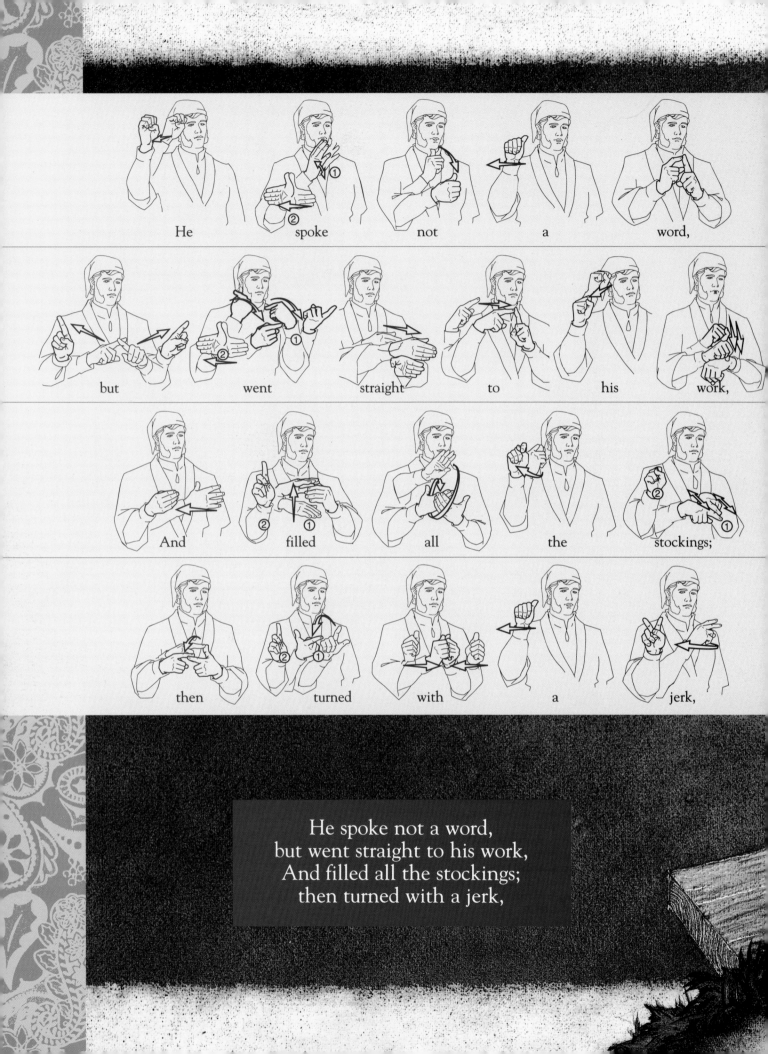

He spoke not a word,
but went straight to his work,
And filled all the stockings;
then turned with a jerk,

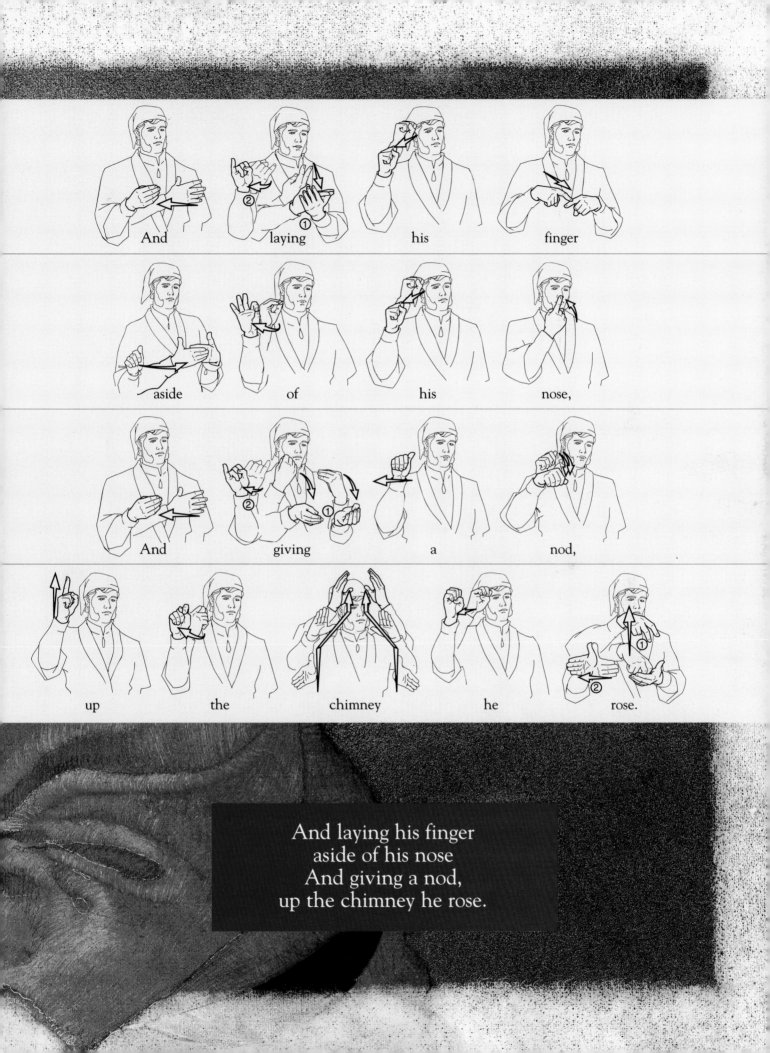

And laying his finger
aside of his nose
And giving a nod,
up the chimney he rose.

He   sprang   to   his   sleigh

to   his   team   gave   a   whistle.

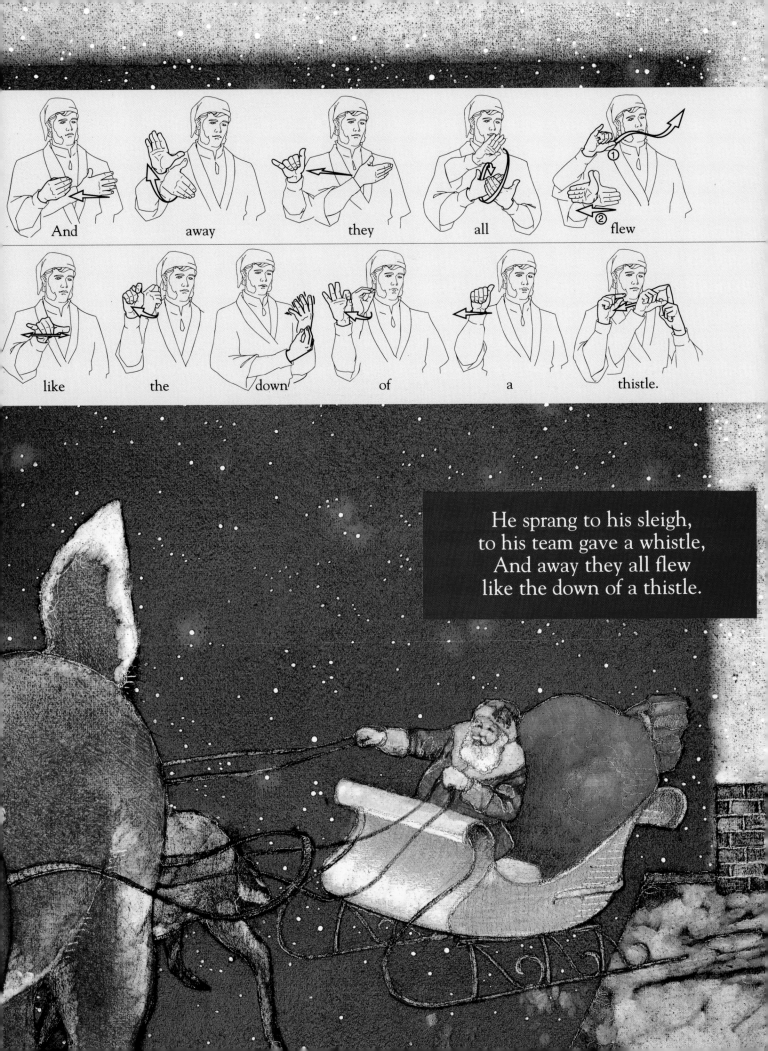

And away they all flew

like the down of a thistle.

He sprang to his sleigh,
to his team gave a whistle,
And away they all flew
like the down of a thistle.

But I heard him exclaim,
as he drove out of sight,
"Happy Christmas to all,
and to all a good night."

But     I     heard     him     exclaim,

as     he     drove     out     of     sight,

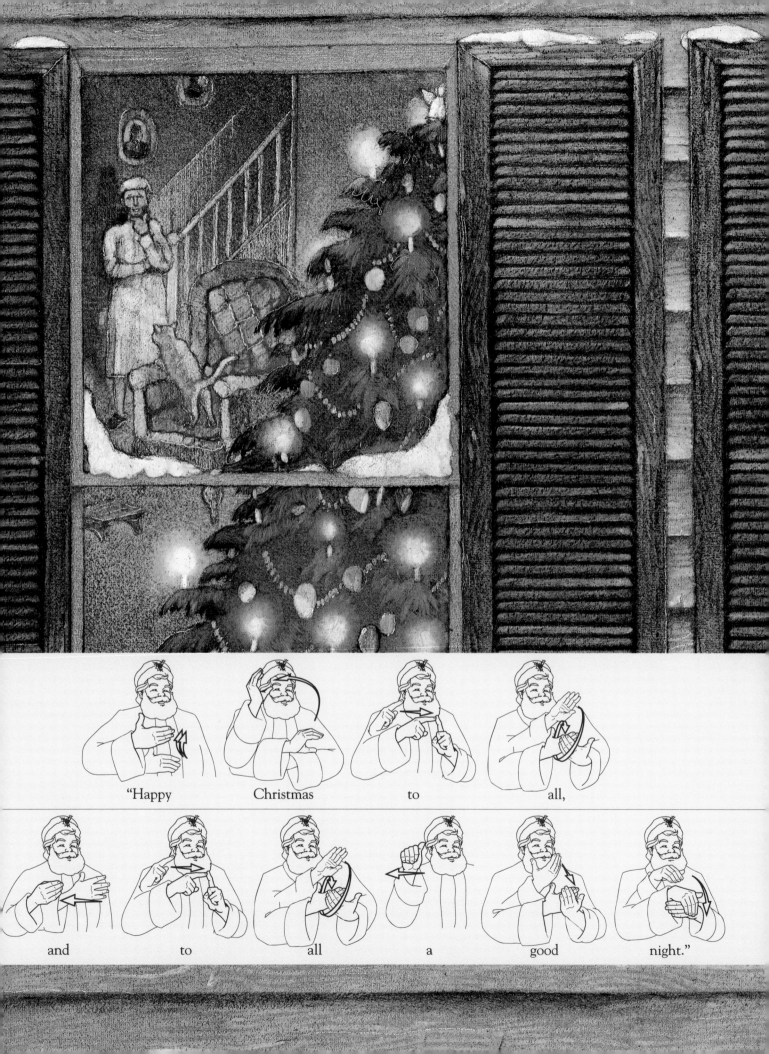

"Happy     Christmas     to     all,

and     to     all     a     good     night."

# Children can learn more about sign language and deafness from the following books and videotapes:

**Discovering Sign Language** *by Laura Greene and Eva B. Dicker.* Children learn all about hearing loss, different sign language systems, games, and "How the Seasons Came to Be," a story in sign for elementary-age children.
*ISBN 0-930323-48-3, 5 1/4" x 8 1/4" softcover, 104 pages, line drawings.*

**I Can Sign My ABCs** *by Susan Chaplin, illustrated by Laura McCaul.* This full-color book has 26 signs, each with its manual alphabet handshape followed by the picture, the name, and the sign for a simple object beginning with that letter, an ideal book for teaching both the English and the American Manual alphabets.
*ISBN 0-930323-19-X, 7" x 7 1/2" hardcover, 56 pages, full-color illustrations.*

**King Midas With Selected Sentences in American Sign Language** *adapted by Robert Newby, illustrated by Dawn Majewski and Sandy Cozzolino.* This classic tale of King Midas, who turns everything he touches into gold, is accompanied by line drawings of 44 selected sentences in American Sign Language, and 120 signs for different vocabulary words.
*ISBN 0-930323-75-0, 8 1/2" x 11" hardcover, 64 pages, full-color illustrations, line drawings.*

**King Midas Videotape,** the companion to the book, features renowned deaf actor Mike Lamitola first explaining in sign language ten key sentences and signs for important vocabulary words. Then, while dressed in full costume, he signs and performs the complete story, showing the full elegance and beauty of American Sign Language.
*ISBN 0-930323-71-8, VHS, 30 minutes, ISBN 0-930323-77-7, book and videotape.*

**Little Red Riding Hood Told in Signed English** *by Harry Bornstein and Karen L. Saulnier, illustrated by Bradley O. Pomeroy.* One of the most loved folktales is told through text and drawings of Signed English, the system that uses American Sign Language signs to give children a strong grasp of English grammar and vocabulary.
*ISBN 0-930323-63-7, 8 1/2" x 11" hardcover, 48 pages, full-color illustrations, line drawings.*

**My First Book of Sign** *by Pamela J. Baker, illustrated by Patricia Bellan Gillen.* This alphabet book gives the signs for the 150 words most frequently used by young children. This text includes explanations on how to form each sign.
*ISBN 0-930323-20-3, 9" x 12" hardcover, full-color illustrations.*

**My Signing Book of Numbers** *by Patricia Bellan Gillen.* Children can learn their numbers in sign language from this book, which has the appropriate number of things or creatures for numbers 0 through 20, 30, 40, 50, 60, 70, 80, 90, 100, and 1,000.
*ISBN 0-930323-37-8, 9" x 12" hardcover, 56 pages, full-color illustrations, line drawings.*

**Now I Understand** *by Gregory S. LaMore, illustrated by Jan Ensing-Keelean.* At first, the new boy's schoolmates don't understand why he never answers their questions, and they become angry. Then, the teacher explains that he is hard of hearing, which helps the children to understand about hearing loss and "mainstreaming."
*ISBN 0-930323-13-0, 5 1/2" x 8 1/2" flexicover, 52 pages, full-color illustrations.*

**Nursery Rhymes from Mother Goose Told in Signed English** *by Harry Bornstein and Karen L. Saulnier, illustrated by Patricia Peters, sign illustrations by Linda Tom.* More than a dozen favorite verses are illustrated in color, and the text also is told through line drawings of Signed English. Children discover the fun of rhyme while also strengthening their language skills.
*ISBN 0-930323-99-8, 8 1/2" x 11" hardcover, 48 pages, full-color illustrations.*

**Silent Observer** *written and illustrated by Christy MacKinnon.* Born in 1889, Christy MacKinnon became deaf at the age of two. After a successful career as a teacher and illustrator, she retired to paint and write of her childhood in 19th-century Nova Scotia. Her book is a wonderful story of a bygone era.
*ISBN 1-56368-022-X, 11" x 8 1/2" hardcover, 48 pages, full-color illustrations.*

**Sleeping Beauty with Selected Sentences in American Sign Language** *adapted by Robert Newby, illustrated by Pat Steiner and Sandra Cozzolino.* A delightful new rendition of the cherished fairy tale of the princess who slept for 100 years is presented in full color accompanied by line drawings of American Sign language for key sentences.
*ISBN 0-930323-97-1, 8 1/2" x 11" hardcover, 64 pages, full-color illustrations, line drawings.*

**Sleeping Beauty Videotape** features deaf actor Rita Corey showing important signs for adjectives from the story, accompanied by illustrations from the book, then signing the story twice in full costume.
*ISBN 0-930323-98-X, VHS, color, running time 30 minutes.*

**A Very Special Friend** *by Dorothy Hoffman Levi, illustrated by Ethel Gold.* Frannie, who is six, finds a very special friend. She meets Laura, who "talks" in sign language. Laura teaches Frannie signing, and they become fast friends.
*ISBN 0-930323-55-6, 8 1/2" x 7" hardcover, 32 pages, full-color illustrations.*

**A Very Special Sister** *by Dorothy Hoffman Levi, illustrated by Ethel Gold.* Laura, who is deaf, hopes that her mother's new baby is a girl. Then Laura begins to worry that her mother will love the baby more if the baby can hear.
*ISBN 0-930323-96-3, 8 1/2" x 7" hardcover, 32 pages, full-color illustrations.*